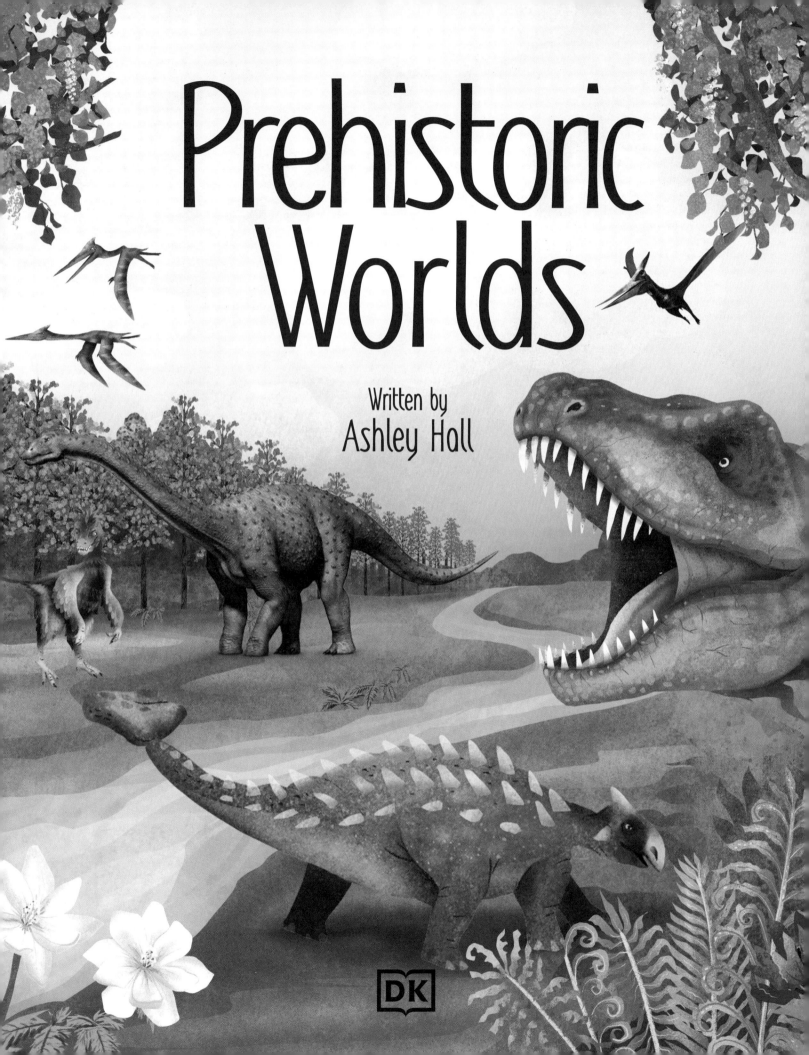

Prehistoric Worlds

Written by
Ashley Hall

DK

Author Ashley Hall
Illustrator Claire McElfatrick
Project Editor Sophie Parkes
Designer Sonny Flynn
US Editor Jill Hamilton
US Senior Editor Shannon Beatty
Editor Sarah MacLeod Bailey
Design Assistant Hannah Moore
Picture Researcher Sakshi Saluja
Senior Production Editor Dragana Puvacic
Production Controller Rebecca Parton
Managing Editor Penny Smith
Deputy Art Director Mabel Chan
Publishing Director Sarah Larter

First American Edition, 2024
Published in the United States by DK Publishing
1745 Broadway, 20th Floor, New York, NY 10019

A catalog record for this book
is available from the Library of Congress.
ISBN 978-0-7440-9186-1

DK books are available at special discounts when
purchased in bulk for sales promotions, premiums,
fund-raising, or educational use.
For details, contact: DK Publishing Special Markets,
1745 Broadway, 20th Floor NY, NY 10019
SpecialSales@dk.com

Printed and bound in China

www.dk.com

MIX
Paper | Supporting
responsible forestry
FSC™ C018179

This book was made with Forest
Stewardship Council™ certified
paper – one small step in DK's
commitment to a sustainable future.
For more information go to
www.dk.com/our-green-pledge

INTRODUCTION

When you think of paleontology, do dinosaurs come to mind? Paleontology is the study of ancient life, and dinosaurs are just one fascinating, weird, and wonderful group of millions of life forms that have evolved on our planet.

When I was little, I was dinosaur-obsessed. Now I'm an adult, I'm still dinosaur-obsessed! As a paleontologist, I share my passion for fossils with schools and visitors in museums. Not only is studying fossils fun, but more importantly, it helps uncover the mysteries of prehistoric Earth, and teaches us how to prevent and preserve our existing fragile ecosystems for the future.

I hope this book sparks your passion for dinosaurs and all things paleontology. Let's "dig in" to the incredible prehistoric worlds together.

Ashley Hall

Ashley Hall

CONTENTS

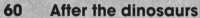

HOW WE STUDY PREHISTORIC WORLDS

The study of ancient life, including animals, plants, fungi, bacteria, and the traces they have left behind, is called paleontology.

Remains of many once-living things have been preserved as fossils. Organisms living today might be preserved as fossils in the future, too.

Paleontologists study prehistoric worlds through discovering and studying fossils.

Read on to find out how fossils can reveal the secrets of Earth's fascinating past.

What is a fossil?

Fossils are the preserved remains of a once-living organism that we can study to learn about prehistoric worlds.

TYPES OF FOSSILIZATION

Fossils can be formed in many different ways. Petrification, the process of minerals filling in where soft tissue used to be, is the most common way fossils are formed. But there are many other ways that dead organisms can be preserved.

Carbonization

Carbonization occurs when an organism is put under tremendous pressure, so it gets preserved as a thin layer of carbon. Plants and fish fossils are often preserved this way.

Petrified wood

Petrification

In this process, water carries microscopic minerals into the remains of an organism, replacing the soft tissue and hardening to form a fossil.

Freezing

Ice Age animals and plants that are thousands of years old can be found frozen in ice with their skin, fur, feathers, and leaves still perfectly preserved.

Silene stenophylla
This plant was grown by scientists from a 32,000-year-old seed found preserved in permafrost!

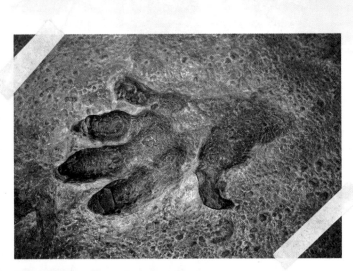

Molds and casts
Natural molds, such as footprints, shells, or plants, can be filled in with sediment, such as sand, mud, or silt, to create 3D impressions.

Dinosaur tail preserved in amber

Amber
Sticky resin oozes from tree branches, trapping anything it touches. It hardens into a substance called amber, preserving insects, spiders, and even small dinosaur parts in perfect condition.

HOW TO BECOME A FOSSIL

Just one percent of all life that has ever lived on Earth was lucky enough to become a fossil, so fossils are very special. Some types are extremely rare.

Step 1
Die and leave a trace behind.

Step 2
Quickly get buried by sand, mud, tar, ice, or sediment from rivers, ponds, or lakes.

Step 3
Lie underground for thousands, hundreds of thousands, millions, or billions of years.

Step 4
Wait for erosion from strong winds, running water, glaciers, or earthquakes to expose you just in time to be discovered by a paleontologist!

CENOZOIC ERA

The Cenozoic Era, or age of mammals, covers the last 66 million years, including the present day. After nonavian dinosaurs went extinct, mammals the size of mice evolved into a huge range of mammals, and fish, birds, reptiles, and more also developed into the animals we see on Earth today.

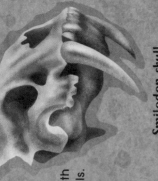

Smilodon skull

Saber-toothed cat
Long, sharp canine teeth helped hunt big animals.

Coronodon skull

Early whale
Coronodon is an early type of whale.

Pakicetus

Early whale ancestor
Whales evolved from small, semiaquatic mammals such as Pakicetus.

Megalodon tooth

Largest shark
Otodus megalodon went extinct as recently as 3 million years ago (MYA).

Holocene
– – – – (10,000 years ago)

Pleistocene
– – – – (1.8 MYA)

Pliocene
– – – – (5.3 MYA)

Miocene
– – – – (23 MYA)

Oligocene
– – – – (33.9 MYA)

Eocene
– – – – (55.8 MYA)

Paleocene
– – – – (65.5 MYA)

MESOZOIC ERA

The Mesozoic Era began after one huge extinction and ended with another. Dinosaurs, pterosaurs, and marine reptiles ruled the Earth for 180 million years.

Noisy dinosaur
Dinosaurs evolved a range of features, such as this crest that made a sound like a tuba.

Parasaurolophus skull Skull

Cretaceous
– – – – (145.5 MYA)

Prehistoric timeline

From Earth's formation 4.6 billion years ago (BYA), history has been preserved in the Earth's layers as fossils. They have told us everything we know about the prehistoric worlds. Here are all the different periods of history we will cover in this book.

Early dinosaur
The first dinosaurs were small, fast, and slender.

Coelophysis skeleton

Allosaurus skull

Predator dinosaur
Allosaurus hunted and ate huge dinosaurs such as Diplodocus.

Jurassic

– – – (199.6 MYA)

Triassic

– – – (252.2 MYA)

PALEOZOIC ERA

The Paleozoic Era was a time of major changes. The first life forms evolved, diversified, and adapted from swimming in the sea to walking on land.

Dimetrodon skull

Marine mollusks
Ammonites, relatives of squid and octopus, grew in these coiled shells.

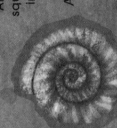

Ammonites

Mammal rulers
Before dinosaurs, large, lizardlike mammals ruled the land.

Echinoderm

Brachiopod

Trilobite

Permian

– – – (299 MYA)

Pennsylvanian

– – – (318 MYA)

Mississippian

– – – (359.2 MYA)

Devonian

– – – (416 MYA)

Silurian

– – – (443 MYA)

Ordovician

– – – (448.3 MYA)

Cambrian

– – – (542 MYA)

PRECAMBRIAN ERA

This is the earliest era in history, starting when Earth formed 4.6 billion years ago! Life on Earth began 3.7 billion years ago or more and continues to this day.

Earliest fossils
The earliest known fossils are microorganisms found in 3.4 billion-year-old Australian chert rocks.

Proterozoic

– – – (2.5 BYA)

Archean

Paleontology needs geology

To find fossils, we first have to study geology, the science of Earth's structure and the processes that act on it. Since Earth's beginning 4.6 billion years ago, layer after layer has formed on Earth's surface like a huge layer cake, creating its crust. You can see different layers of rocks exposed in different parts of the world. We call these various layers "formations."

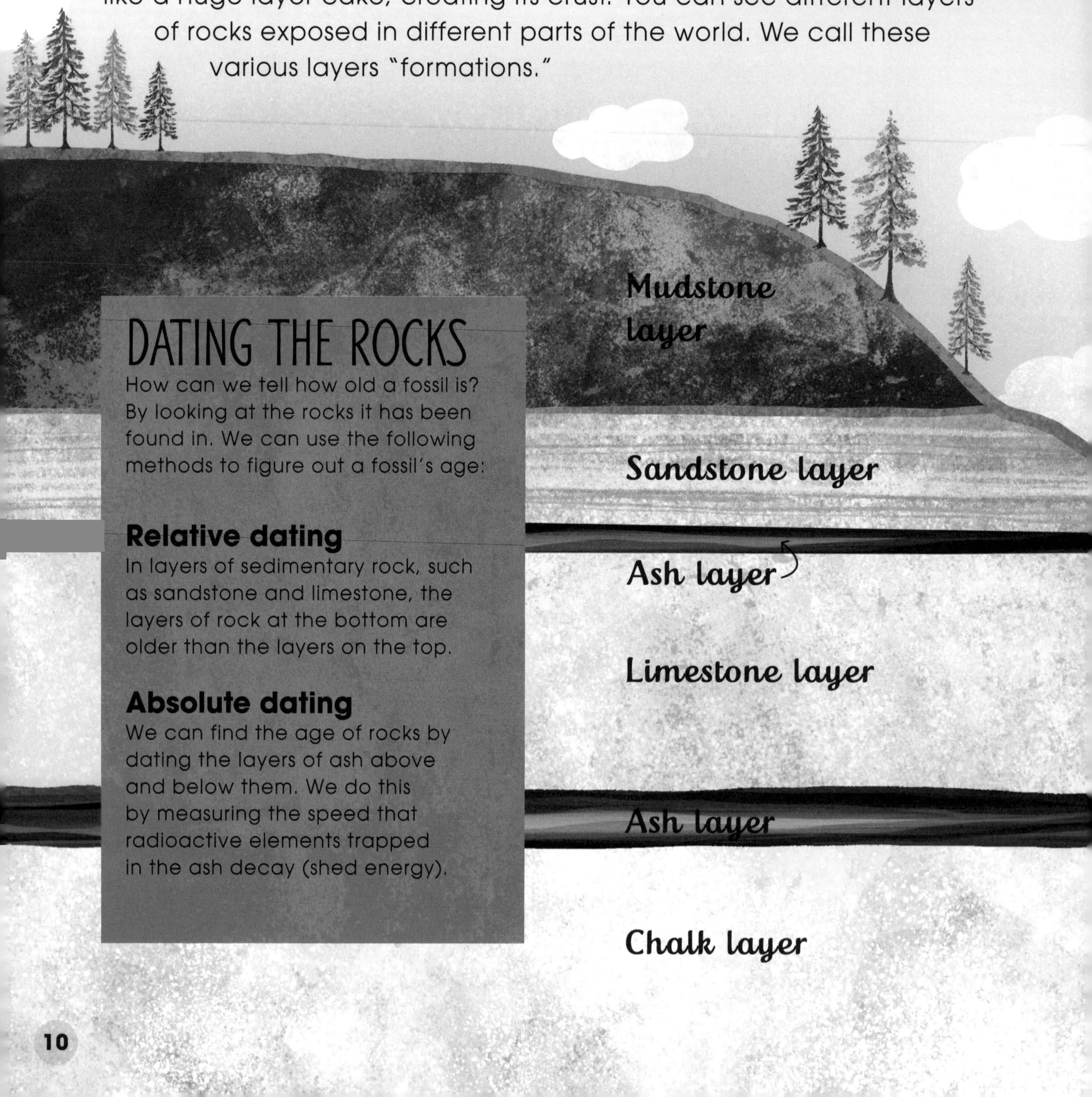

DATING THE ROCKS

How can we tell how old a fossil is? By looking at the rocks it has been found in. We can use the following methods to figure out a fossil's age:

Relative dating

In layers of sedimentary rock, such as sandstone and limestone, the layers of rock at the bottom are older than the layers on the top.

Absolute dating

We can find the age of rocks by dating the layers of ash above and below them. We do this by measuring the speed that radioactive elements trapped in the ash decay (shed energy).

Mudstone layer

Sandstone layer

Ash layer

Limestone layer

Ash layer

Chalk layer

Evolution

Studying geology and fossils can help us understand how life has changed over time. This process is called evolution, and it is a natural, observable part of life that is still happening today. Scientists study evolution to understand how all life on Earth is connected, as all living things evolved from a common ancestor.

"From so simple a beginning, endless forms most beautiful and most wonderful have been, and are being, evolved."
Charles Darwin

OUR EVOLVING EARTH

Although we can't see them move, Earth's continents have been in motion for billions of years. They shift 0.04–0.8 in (1–20 mm) a year in a process called plate tectonics.

251 MYA
In the Triassic, all continents were joined together in one supercontinent called Pangea. Animals could travel across it.

150 MYA
In the Jurassic, Pangea broke apart, creating two huge continents: Laurasia and Gondwana. Seas filled with life cut between them.

66 MYA
In the Cretaceous, continents were in almost the same position as they are today. Some were covered in water.

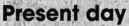

Present day
There are seven continents and five oceans. Scientists think another supercontinent will form in 200–300 million years.

Not everything is a dinosaur!

As you read this book, remember that not all extinct creatures are dinosaurs. Sometimes people use the word "dinosaur" to describe any extinct animal, when actually dinosaurs are their own special group of animals.

Pteranodon

Flying reptile
Pterosaurs are a branch of flying reptiles that existed at the same time as dinosaurs during the Mesozoic Era.

Woolly mammoth

Elephant ancestor
These large Ice Age mammals are closely related to African and Asian elephants.

Saber-toothed cat

Prehistoric cat
Saber-toothed cats, or Smilodon, are Ice Age mammals that are closely related to cats.

Mosasaurus

Swimming reptile
Mosasaurs are marine reptiles more closely related to snakes and monitor lizards than dinosaurs.

We are not dinosaurs
Many creatures, including swimming and flying reptiles, existed alongside dinosaurs. While dinosaurs look like some of these animals, they are a separate group.

Strange wings

The dinosaur Yi qi's batlike wings were made from membranes (strong skin) instead of feathers.

Yi qi

Black-billed magpie

We are dinosaurs

Dinosaurs, including Parasaurolophus and Styracosaurus, are a specialized group of reptiles that evolved in the Mesozoic Era.

Are birds dinosaurs?

Birds are living dinosaurs! They were the only dinosaurs to survive the extinction event 66 million years ago.

Styracosaurus

Parasaurolophus

What is a dinosaur?

Dinosaurs are all related and share the same characteristics: an upright stance with their legs underneath their body, not sprawling out to the side, two holes in the skull behind the eyes, and the ability to lay eggs like other reptiles and birds.

Tyrannosaurus rex

Stegosaurus

Plated lizard

The armored dinosaur Stegosaurus lived 150 million years ago in the Jurassic Period.

Lizard king

T. rex is a dinosaur that lived 66 million years ago in the Late Cretaceous Period.

PALEOZOIC ERA

Around 538 to 252 million years ago, the Paleozoic Era saw life evolve into lots of successful groups of animals. Many are still with us today, such as fish and reptiles.

The era began with an important event known as the Cambrian explosion, when small, single-celled ocean organisms began evolving into **strange, new, complex life forms**, such as the trilobites shown here. Hard-shelled trilobites were so successful that they existed in the world's oceans for 270 million years before dying out in a mass extinction.

Read on to learn all about the Paleozoic Era, **an exciting time for reptile evolution.**

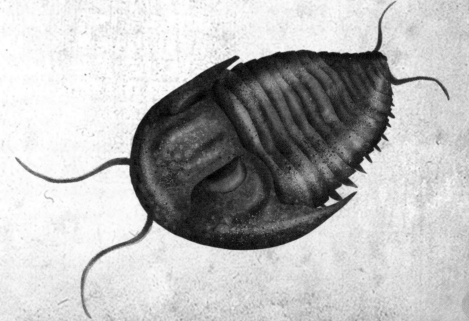

Permian Period

The Permian Period, 298 to 252 million years ago, was a time of great change for Earth. Life evolved rapidly and continents slowly joined together into one giant supercontinent called Pangea.

Life before dinosaurs
In this time before dinosaurs evolved, Dimetrodon and other large reptiles were Earth's top predators.

Dimetrodon

Diplocaulus

Eryops

Water to land
Amphibians evolved from fish, developing lungs and bony-limbed fins. In the Permian, amphibians such as giant Eryops and boomerang-headed Diplocaulus lived both on land and in water.

Two horns
Diplocaulus had a skull with two horns. Bite marks found in its fossilized skull have taught us that Dimetrodon would hunt Diplocaulus, dragging it from its burrow by its snout.

Diplocaulus

Meganeura

Giant insects
Meganeura was a giant dragonfly with a wingspan of 28 in (71 cm). It buzzed overhead, catching bugs and other invertebrates.

Life on land
The Permian climate was wet and swampy near the coasts and dry on land—ideal conditions for reptiles were able to thrive. Edaphosaurus and Cotylorhynchus were some of the earliest known large herbivorous reptiles.

Edaphosaurus

Cotylorhynchus

Araeoscelis

Dinosaur relatives
Araeoscelis is one of the earliest known diapsids—a group of small, lizardlike reptiles that are closely related to dinosaurs.

Dimetrodon

With a large sail along its back and a mouth packed with sharp, jagged teeth, Dimetrodon is one of the most iconic prehistoric animals ever discovered. At approximately 12 ft (3.5 m) long and weighing up to 400 lb (180 kg), this reptile was one of the Permian Period's top predators.

Dimetrodon was a meat-eater that hunted freshwater sharks and amphibians.

What was the sail for?...

Tough teeth

Dimetrodon means "two measures of teeth." It had both sharp, slicing teeth and serrated (bumpy-edged) teeth, which helped it tear through tough meat.

Nasty bite
Scientists have found bite marks from Dimetrodon teeth on the bones of other Dimetrodon!

...Paleontologists are still puzzled!

Dimetrodon was one of the first animals to have serrated teeth.

What am I?
Believe it or not, Dimetrodon is more closely related to you than to dinosaurs! Both mammals (like you) and Dimetrodon are synapsids: a group of animals with four limbs and one hole behind each eye socket.

Tall sail
Elongated back bones made up the sail, which may have been used to attract mates or scare off other males.

Swamp-dweller
Dimetrodon was adapted to a range of habitats, but was mostly found in wetlands.

Paleozoic oceans

Panthalassa, the ocean that surrounded Pangea, was full of strange and wonderful creatures that evolved during the Paleozoic Era. This was a time where simple, single-celled organisms evolved into more complex animals.

The male falcatus had a large, forward-pointing spine on its head.

Falcatus

CAMBRIAN EXPLOSION

This exciting time on Earth is known as the Cambrian explosion. All major groups of animals evolved during this 13–25-million-year period. It was during this time that the first eyes, early backbones, gills, and mouths evolved.

Stethacanthus

This fish had a strange-shaped dorsal fin, covered with rows of scaly denticles (teethlike bumps). The use of these is unknown.

Helicoprion

This sharklike fish is known for its nightmarish, spiraling whorl of teeth. This was probably used to pull soft prey into its mouth.

Fossil of Helicoprion teeth

MARINE CREATURES

In the Cambrian explosion, marine invertebrates—animals without backbones such as mollusks and arthropods—evolved and thrived. Animals that were once soft-bodied developed legs, complex eyes, armor, and ways to protect themselves. Vertebrates such as fish and sharks filled the seas as well.

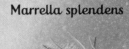

Marrella splendens

Marrella splendens

This strange early arthropod is the most common fossil found at the Burgess Shale area in Canada. More than 25,000 specimens have been collected.

Goniatite

Soliclymenia

Crinoids

Corals

Soliclymenia

Part of the mollusk family (which includes octopus and snails), Soliclymenia is an early ammonite—an extinct shelled animal. Its shell is coiled into an irregular shape.

Brachiopods

Tiktaalik roseae

FIRST LEGS ON LAND

Tetrapods, such as this Tiktaalik roseae, were four-limbed vertebrates that could pull themselves onto land. They evolved from fish 385 million years ago. All tetrapods, including dinosaurs, amphibians, lizards, and mammals, evolved from these aquatic ancestors.

Limbs were used to climb up onto land.

Estemmenosuchus

Estemmenosuchus means "crowned crocodile" in Greek, although they are not related to crocodiles. So what were these strange Permian creatures? Though they looked like a cross between a dinosaur, a pig, and a crocodile, they were actually therapsids— distant cousins of modern-day mammals.

Swamp swimmer
Estemmenosuchus could have spent time in marshes and swamps due to its hippolike skin.

Osteoderm

Bumpy skin surface

Skin, scales, or fur?
Skin impressions discovered from the face of Estemmenosuchus show that it had skin like a hairless mammal—not scales. Osteoderms (tiny embedded bones) made the skin bumpy.

Defensive horns
Two large horns may have been used for display or defense.

Sharp teeth
Large, sharp canine teeth were most likely used for fighting.

TERRIBLE HEADS

Estemmenosuchus were Permian therapsids called dinocephalians, which means "terrible heads." This was due to bumps, horns, and protrusions on their huge skulls.

Adult Estemmenosuchus could grow to be 10 ft (3 m) long— larger than a cow!

Meat and plant eater
Estemmenosuchus was an omnivore, eating both meat and plants.

Strong fighter

Its squat, sprawling posture and large, muscular shoulders made this therapsid strong, possibly for fighting with prey or other Estemmenosuchus.

Permian plants

Plants of the Permian Period were an important source of food for land animals.
Tall lycopod trees, lush ferns, and horsetails filled the Permian swamps, while ginkgos and conifers thrived in drier places.

Seed fern

Horsetail

Ginkgo

Lycopod

Conifer

Cycad

Living fossils
Though many of these plants look other-worldly, most of these groups have survived every extinction. Their descendants still exist on Earth today as "living fossils."

CONIFERS

Conifers, or pine trees, such as Walchia grew tall and created shaded canopies in drier regions.

GINKGOS

Nonflowering ginkgos reproduce by spreading seeds, and share a common ancestor with cycads.

Studying fossils of the seed fern Glossopteris helped scientists discover that all of Earth's continents used to be connected as one supercontinent called Gondwana.

CYCADS

Cycads have woody trunks with crowns of large, stiff leaves. They still exist in forests today.

HORSETAILS

Horsetails include Calamites—extinct treelike plants that could grow as tall as 160 ft (50 m).

SEED FERNS

Seed ferns were the first group of plants to produce seeds instead of spores to reproduce.

LYCOPODS

Lycopods such as Lepidodendron grew to heights of 160 ft (50 m). Leaves grew from their trunks.

The Great Dying

In the largest mass extinction ever on Earth, the Permian-Triassic extinction (nicknamed the Great Dying), an incredible 90 percent of all marine life and 70 percent of all life on land was wiped out.

Meganeura

Moschops

Inostrancevia

Dimetrodon

What went extinct?

As Earth became hotter and drier, forests disappeared, as well as the animals that relied on forest plants for food and shelter. Most large reptiles went extinct, while small and adaptable living things survived.

The Permian–Triassic extinction

The Great Dying occurred at the end of the Permian Period, 252 million years ago. Unlike the extinction at the end of the Cretaceous Period, which caused the dinosaurs (except birds) to die off suddenly, the Permian-Triassic extinction happened slowly and gradually due to the changing climate.

Volcanic eruptions from the Siberian Traps may be one major cause of this extinction.

The whole extinction lasted from **3 to 15 million years.**

Plant life
Plants may have been the first species to suffer the effects of this extinction event.

Pleuromeia

Lystrosaurus

The great survivor
Lystrosaurus could burrow, which may have helped it survive the event.

What survived?
Lystrosaurus, a small dicynodont therapsid (a mammal-like reptile), survived, as well as cynodont therapsids: a group that includes the ancestors of mammals. Survivors withstood the toxic environment, giving rise to a new group of animals—dinosaurs.

What was the cause?
The Great Dying was caused by climate change, after carbon dioxide was released from huge volcanic eruptions in the Siberian Traps in what is now Russia. This carbon dioxide caused Earth's temperature to increase and the oceans to become more acidic, making it impossible for many living things to survive.

Dueling dinosaurs
T. rex and Triceratops are on display at the Natural History Museum of Los Angeles County (NHMLA) in the US.

THE AGE OF DINOSAURS

After the Permian-Triassic extinction, life recovered slowly and a new group of animals evolved: dinosaurs. They would evolve to be the largest land animals the world had ever seen.

Dinosaurs first evolved 250 million years ago and thrived for 180 million years. Thanks to paleontology, we can now find bones, footprints, coprolites (fossil poo), eggs, and many more kinds of dinosaur fossils in museums all around the world.

Read on to learn all about **the fascinating world of the dinosaurs.**

Mesozoic Era

The Mesozoic Era is divided up into three different time periods—why? Because each end of a period represents an extinction event, when many groups of animals and plants went extinct and new forms of life evolved in their place. There were three extinctions during the Mesozoic Era and each happened for a different reason.

Three of the five largest mass extinctions of all time happened during the Mesozoic Era.

TRIASSIC PERIOD

Dinosaur beginnings (252–201 MYA)

Very few animals survived the Permian-Triassic extinction. With these animals gone, others were able to evolve in their place in the Triassic Period. Dinosaurs evolved from small, bipedal (two-legged) archosaurs and the first marine reptiles appeared. The period ended with climate change caused by volcanic eruptions.

Plateosaurus

Silesaurus

Herrerasaurus

Ichthyosaurus

JURASSIC PERIOD

Pterodactylus

The time of giants (201–145 MYA)

The supercontinent Pangea divided. Ichthyosaurs and plesiosaurs dominated the sea, sauropod dinosaurs the land, and pterosaurs the sky. Small mammals and birds evolved. Climate change and declining oxygen in the oceans, or anoxia, marked the end of the Jurassic Period.

Brachiosaurus

Stegosaurus

Allosaurus

CRETACEOUS PERIOD

The final dinosaur era (145–66 MYA)

Dinosaurs of all shapes and sizes, from the smallest theropod, Microraptor, to the largest sauropod, Patagotitan, evolved. Flowering plants appeared too. Dinosaurs, pterosaurs, marine reptiles, and plants could be found on every continent in the world, including Antarctica. The final time period for nonavian dinosaurs lasted for 79 million years until the final Mesozoic extinction, the K-Pg extinction.

Microraptor

Velociraptor

Patagotitan

Iguanodon

Rain showers bring...dinosaurs?

In the late Triassic, 234–232 million years ago, the climate went from being dry and hot to very wet in an event called the Carnian Pluvial Episode. Volcanic eruptions in Canada released huge amounts of greenhouse gases, which warmed the Earth and caused rain to fall worldwide for 1–2 million years. As a result of this event, plants thrived and dinosaurs diversified.

Triassic animals

In the Permian-Triassic extinction event, climate change meant the air and water became harmful to all living things. During the Triassic Period that followed, the air cleared and life recovered. The first mammals, dinosaurs, and pterosaurs (flying reptiles) evolved.

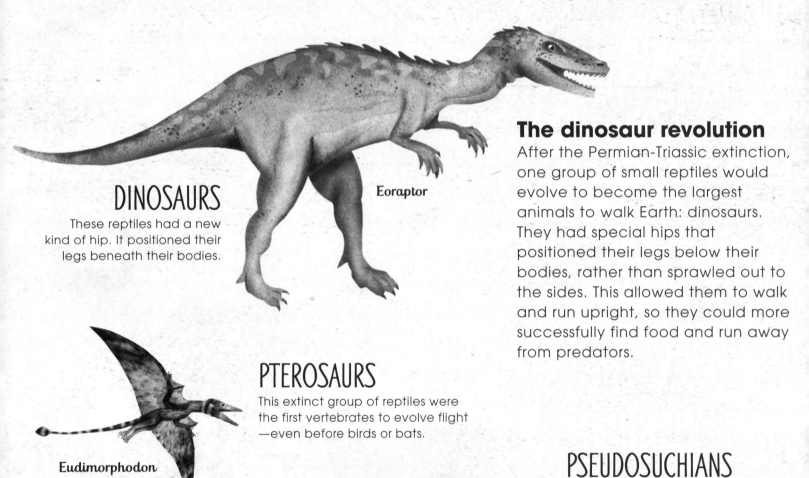

Eoraptor

Eudimorphodon

Phytosaur

DINOSAURS

These reptiles had a new kind of hip. It positioned their legs beneath their bodies.

The dinosaur revolution

After the Permian-Triassic extinction, one group of small reptiles would evolve to become the largest animals to walk Earth: dinosaurs. They had special hips that positioned their legs below their bodies, rather than sprawled out to the sides. This allowed them to walk and run upright, so they could more successfully find food and run away from predators.

PTEROSAURS

This extinct group of reptiles were the first vertebrates to evolve flight —even before birds or bats.

PSEUDOSUCHIANS

These archosaurs include aetosaurs, phytosaurs, and poposaurs. They are closely related to modern crocodiles.

ARCHOSAURS

The name "archosaur" means "ruling lizard." Archosaurs are a diverse group of reptiles that includes the ancestors of birds and crocodiles. Birds and crocodilians are now the only living archosaurs left on Earth.

Ericiolacerta

Mammal origins
Many of the features that we see in mammals today were originally found in therapsids, such as having four limbs located underneath the body.

Siriusgnathus

Elephantosaurus

THERAPSIDS
Mammals evolved from this strange group 201 million years ago. Being small, nocturnal, and able to control their body temperature helped therapsids to survive.

The Triassic Period was a time of recovery and great change.

Peltobatrachus

Eryops

Gerrothorax

TEMNOSPONDYLS
This group of large amphibians were relatives of modern frogs and salamanders. They were some of the first vertebrates to adapt to life on land 330 million years ago.

Morganucodon

Little beast
Morganucodon was just 4 in (10 cm) long and looked like a mouse or shrew.

TRUE MAMMALS
Small, furry, and no bigger than mice, mammals evolved 201 million years ago from therapsids. Mammals are the only therapsids still living on Earth today.

Megalancosaurus

Life in the trees
Drepanosaurs had tails that could wrap around branches, and some had thumblike toes for grasping.

Drepanosaurus

DREPANOSAURS
These early reptiles were not chameleons, but they looked like them! They had similar adaptations for living in the trees and feeding on insects and other small animals.

EARTH'S FIRST GIANT

Cymbospondylus was a reptile called an ichthyosaur that lived 244 million years ago. The largest creature of its time, it grew to the size of a sperm whale— a whopping 56 ft (17 m) long.

Cymbospondylus youngorum

Ammonites

Triassic oceans

After the Permian-Triassic extinction that wiped out many animal groups, a wide range of reptiles came to thrive in the Triassic oceans. They evolved features like webbed feet and paddlelike tails to become successful hunters and dominate the waters.

Food fit for a giant
Cymbospondylus reached its huge size by eating ammonites, fish, squid, and maybe even other smaller marine reptiles.

Nothosaurus

These marine reptiles were 13 ft (4 m) long. With their webbed feet and long, slender bodies, these Triassic fish-hunters may have had a similar lifestyle to seals and sea lions.

Nothosaurus

Atopodentatus

Atopodentatus

These were some of the first marine herbivores, eating algae from the sandy seabed with their rows of zipperlike, needle-shaped teeth. The first Atopodentatus fossil was discovered in China in 2014.

Ichthyosaurs had a **powerful tail** for swimming.

During the Triassic Period, most of the land on Earth formed a huge landmass surrounded by ocean.

On the menu
Squishy, squidlike belemnites were an important food source for many marine animals.

Belemnites

Valley of the Moon

San Juan in Argentina has one of the world's best sites for early Triassic fossils: Valle de la Luna, or Valley of the Moon, named for its moonlike appearance. The oldest dinosaur fossils have been discovered in the Ischigualasto Formation, which has been dated to 227 million years old.

First dinosaurs
The valley was home to some of the earliest dinosaurs known to have existed.

LANDSCAPE OF THE PAST

This hot, dry land was once a lush floodplain. Lots of rain meant rushing rivers and rich greenery. Herrerasaurus, Eoraptor, Pisanosaurus, aetosaurs, dicynodonts, amphibians, rhynchosaurs, and cynodonts ruled.

Rhynchosaur

An extraordinary fossil site

Over time, the valley was covered in ash from volcanic eruptions, which preserved a huge range of living things as fossils. These included 130 ft (40 m) tall tree trunks of Protojuniperoxylon ischigualastianus trees, reptiles such as Rhynchosaurs, and dinosaurs such as Eoraptor.

Plant-eaters

Rhynchosaurs were 3–6 ft (1–2 m) long, plant-eating reptiles with powerful beaks, large tooth plates, and massive claws for digging.

WIND FORMATIONS

Over time, the sandstone and mudstone landscape of Ischigualasto Provincial Park has been carved into amazing rock formations by wind. This has revealed the layers of the rock laid down by rivers in the Triassic Period.

Layered rock

Paleontologists look for fossils preserved in rock layers called strata.

Herrerasaurus bones were first discovered here in 1958.

Discovering Herrerasaurus

This is one of the earliest known dinosaurs from the fossil record. For years, scientists didn't know if it was a dinosaur, because only a few of its fossils had been found. With the discovery of an almost complete skeleton and skull in Ischigualasto Provincial Park in 1988, Herrerasaurus was officially classified as a saurischian dinosaur.

Herrerasaurus

Jurassic Period

In the Jurassic Period, Pangea slowly split into two separate continents called Laurasia and Gondwana. Volcanic activity made the climate warmer and more tropical across the globe. Dinosaurs evolved and diversified into a variety of shapes and sizes.

Suit of armour
Thyreophorans, such as the Gargoyleosaurus, had thick plates of bone embedded in their skin.

Gargoyleosaurus

Evolution of defense

As carnivorous dinosaurs grew larger, some herbivorous dinosaurs evolved defenses to protect themselves. Dinosaurs with armor were more likely to survive attacks and pass on successful traits to their young. Over time, their spikes and armor grew larger and stronger.

Defensive spikes
Sharp, thick tail spikes were used as weapons against Allosaurus and Ceratosaurus.

Stegosaurus

Jurassic giants

Types of long-necked dinosaurs called sauropods were the largest land animals on Earth. They grew to enormous sizes, allowing them to reach trees higher in the canopy than all other herbivores. Their size kept predators away.

Apatosaurus

Long neck
Brachiosaurus was adapted to eating leaves high up in the canopy.

Ancient glider
This early mammal had thin skin between its limbs for gliding.

Brachiosaurus

Volaticotherium

Early mammal
The tiny gliding Volaticotherium was a 200-million-year-old mammal from China. It is one of the earliest known mammals and one of our earliest relatives.

Mammals diversify

In the Jurassic Period, mammals started to diversify (become more varied) from their Triassic relatives. Beaverlike mammals called Castorocauda and small, rodentlike mammals called multituberculates thrived in this time.

Minibeast
Tiny Hadrocodium was the size of a paperclip.

Megazostrodon

Mouse-sized mammal
The 4 in (10 cm)-long Megazostrodon had rodentlike fur and teeth.

Hadrocodium

Yi qi

Is it a dragon, a bat, or a bird? None of these! Yi qi, meaning "strange wing," is part of a group of dinosaurs called scansoriopterygids. While long arms, extended fingers, and perching feet had been discovered in other dinosaurs, scansoriopterygids were the first to have wings made from a layer of skin called a membrane.

Teeth
Yi qi had small teeth only in the front of its snout.

Just one fossil specimen of Yi qi has been found.

An unusual dinosaur
Scansoriopterygids were an unusual group of dinosaurs adapted to life in the trees. While they had wings, they were only able to glide. They are the smallest known nonflying dinosaurs—Yi qi is just the size of a pigeon.

Wing fingers
Yi qi had three fingers that helped it climb and grab prey.

Wings
The wings were made of a thin membrane of skin, like the wings of a bat.

Wing support
This extra-long bony extension is an adaptation that helps support the wing membrane.

Feathers
Most of Yi qi's body had a thick covering of feathers. It may have had long tail feathers, helping it balance while gliding.

Clawed feet
Curved claws helped Yi qi grasp onto branches and grab prey.

THE EVOLUTION OF FLIGHT

Flight has evolved across several different groups of vertebrates: birds, bats, pterosaurs, and scansoriopterygids. Each group evolved wings from their hand and arm bones. The same bones in each wing are highlighted below.

Birds

Fingers

Forearm

Upper arm

Bats

Pterosaurs

Scansoriopterygids

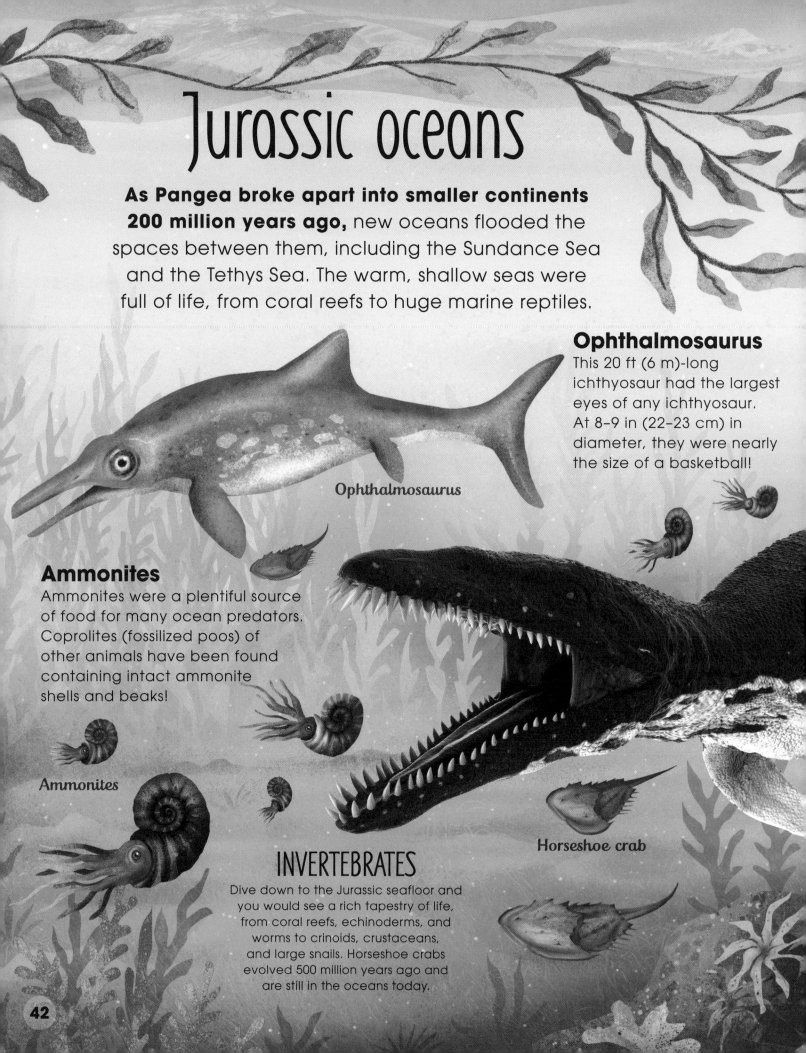

Jurassic oceans

As Pangea broke apart into smaller continents 200 million years ago, new oceans flooded the spaces between them, including the Sundance Sea and the Tethys Sea. The warm, shallow seas were full of life, from coral reefs to huge marine reptiles.

Ophthalmosaurus
This 20 ft (6 m)-long ichthyosaur had the largest eyes of any ichthyosaur. At 8–9 in (22–23 cm) in diameter, they were nearly the size of a basketball!

Ophthalmosaurus

Ammonites
Ammonites were a plentiful source of food for many ocean predators. Coprolites (fossilized poos) of other animals have been found containing intact ammonite shells and beaks!

Ammonites

INVERTEBRATES
Dive down to the Jurassic seafloor and you would see a rich tapestry of life, from coral reefs, echinoderms, and worms to crinoids, crustaceans, and large snails. Horseshoe crabs evolved 500 million years ago and are still in the oceans today.

Horseshoe crab

Leedsichthys

This 66 ft (20 m)-long fish gulped down plankton (tiny plants and animals) by swimming with its mouth wide open, taking in food and filtering out water.

Belemnites

These squidlike animals grabbed their fish prey with hooks on their tentacles. To escape predators, they squirted black ink and darted away.

Liopleurodon

The 22 ft (6.6 m)-long Liopleurodon is a pliosaur—a plesiosaur with a short neck and large jaws. It would hunt other large marine animals, including ichthyosaurs.

Leedsichthys

Belemnite

Liopleurodon

Sponge

Coral

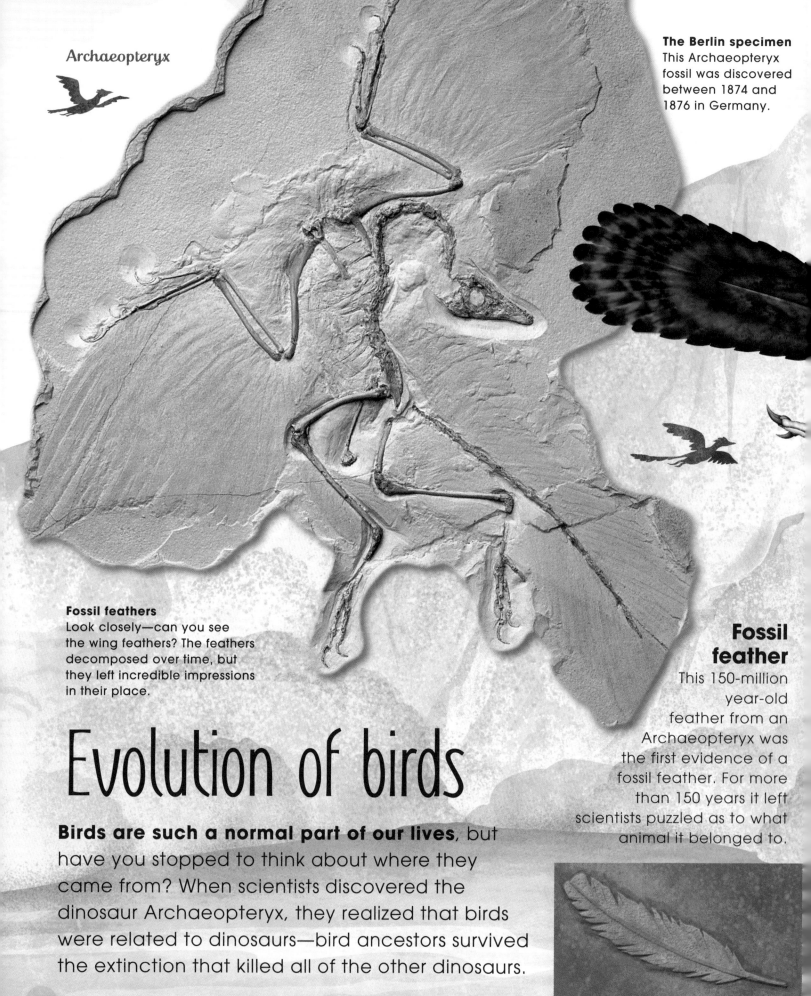

Archaeopteryx

Fossil feathers
Look closely—can you see the wing feathers? The feathers decomposed over time, but they left incredible impressions in their place.

Fossil feather
This 150-million year-old feather from an Archaeopteryx was the first evidence of a fossil feather. For more than 150 years it left scientists puzzled as to what animal it belonged to.

Evolution of birds

Birds are such a normal part of our lives, but have you stopped to think about where they came from? When scientists discovered the dinosaur Archaeopteryx, they realized that birds were related to dinosaurs—bird ancestors survived the extinction that killed all of the other dinosaurs.

Dinosaur or bird?

Archaeopteryx had a long, bony tail, three fingers on each leg, teeth like a dinosaur, and feathers and hollow bones like a bird. This blend of features make Archaeopteryx a transitional fossil between bird and dinosaur!

Useful features
Feathers helped it fly, stay warm, and attract a mate.

Archaeopteryx

FEATHERED DINOSAURS

Since Archaeopteryx's discovery, lots more feathered theropod dinosaurs have been found, many of which in China.

Velociraptor

Sinosauropteryx

Discovering fossil color

Scientists use high-powered microscopes to scan fossil feathers for structures called melanosomes. These tiny structures contain the pigment responsible for color in skin, hair, feathers, and more.

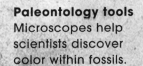

Paleontology tools
Microscopes help scientists discover color within fossils.

Dinosaurs among us

Birds, or avian dinosaurs, survived the mass extinction, so now there are over 10,000 species of dinosaurs living among us all around the world!

Ostrich

45

The Jurassic Coast

With towering cliffs of gray shale full of Jurassic Period treasures, the area around Lyme Regis in Dorset, UK, is one of the most famous fossil-rich sites in the world. These cliffs, known as the Jurassic Coast, hold millions of fossil ammonites, ichthyosaurs, and plesiosaurs, which tumble onto the beaches below.

Jurassic cliffs
These cliffs of shale and limestone are full of 200-million-year-old Jurassic sea creatures.

Famous fossil finder

Mary Anning grew up in Lyme Regis in the 1800s. To help make money for her family, she collected and sold fossils to tourists. In 1811, aged just 12, Mary discovered the first ichthyosaur skeleton near her home. At this time, women were not allowed to be members of the Geological Society, so she had to read as many scientific papers as she could to educate herself.

Pterosaurs

Aged 29, Mary found Dimorphodon, the first pterosaur discovery in England. This specimen can be seen at the Natural History Museum in London, UK.

Dimorphodon macronyx

Ichthyosaurs

Aged 12, Mary found the first ichthyosaur skeleton. Fish bones and scales from its last meal are still inside the ribcage!

Ichthyosaurus anningae

Fossilized fish
Mary found this very well preserved fossil around 1828.

Dapedium politum

MARY'S DISCOVERIES

Mary made more discoveries in her young life than most paleontologists today. Her discoveries helped prove that Earth was much older than was thought at the time, and that there was an age of reptiles before mammals.

Coprolites
Fossilized poo, called coprolite, is a common find on the Jurassic Coast.

Ammonites
Once called snakestones, ammonites are relatives of squid.

Plesiosaurs

Mary found the first plesiosaur skeleton the world had ever seen. Rhomaleosaurus was a pliosaur, a type of plesiosaur. With a long neck and a mouth full of sharp teeth, it was a top predator in the Jurassic seas.

Rhomaleosaurus cramptoni

Belemnites
These mollusk fossils were known as "devil's fingers."

Nyassasaurus

Eoraptor

Lizard hips
The hips point down and forward.

SAURISCHIANS
("lizard-hipped" dinosaurs)

The saurischians were dinosaurs that were more closely related to birds than to Triceratops. Many had hip bones similar to lizards.

THE FIRST DINOSAURS

Appearing in the early Triassic, 245 million years ago, the first dinosaurs were small and bipedal (two-legged). Over millions of years, they evolved and spread into different groups, or families.

Hypsilophodon

Bird hips
The hips point down and backward.

ORNITHISCHIANS
("bird-hipped" dinosaurs)

Despite their birdlike hips, ornithischians were dinosaurs that were more closely related to Triceratops than birds.

Thyreophorans

Dinosaur classification

Classification is arranging or sorting things into groups based on their similarities or differences. Classifying all the different dinosaurs in this way helps us to learn more about their origins and evolution, and to better understand which dinosaurs are related to one another.

Diplodocus

Sauropodomorphs
("lizard feet")
Sauropodomorphs were herbivorous (plant-eating), quadrupedal (four-legged) dinosaurs with small heads, long necks, and leaf-shaped teeth.

Pachycephalosaurus

Pachycephalosaurs
("thick-headed lizards")
Pachycephalosaurs were herbivorous, bipedal dinosaurs famous for their thick skulls surrounded by nodes or spikes.

Allosaurus

Theropods
("beast feet")
These carnivorous (meat-eating), bipedal dinosaurs had hollow bones and small arms. All modern birds are theropods.

Marginocephalians

Triceratops

Gigantspinosaurus

Stegosaurs
("roof lizards")
Stegosaurs were herbivorous, quadrupedal dinosaurs. They were covered in bony plates and spikes for defense against predators.

Ceratopsians
("horned faces")
Ceratopsians were herbivorous, beaked dinosaurs that were once two-legged in the late Jurassic. But over millions of years, they became mostly four-legged.

Ankylosaurus

Ankylosaurs
("rigid lizards")
These herbivorous, quadrupedal dinosaurs had large, clubbed tails and thick armor for defense against predators.

Iguanodon

Ornithopods
("bird feet")
Ornithopods were herbivorous, bipedal dinosaurs with beaks and teeth adapted for eating plants.

Parasaurolophus's **skull** could grow to **5 ft (1.6 m) long!**

Long tail
A long tail helped it balance when standing on its hind legs.

What did it eat?
Plants, please! Leaves, twigs, and pine needles were on the menu for these large herbivores. Thousands of flattened teeth in their jaws, called dental batteries, helped them chew through tough plants.

Pine needles

Parasaurolophus

Duck-billed dinosaurs, known as hadrosaurs, are large herbivores that lived during the late Cretaceous Period. The hadrosaur Parasaurolophus was most known for its unusual head crest, and fossils have been found across North America—from New Mexico, US, to Alberta, Canada.

What was the crest for?

Parasaurolophus had a very interesting and unique skull. The large crest was a hollow chamber used for making sound, but we are still not sure why sounds were made. Computer modeling shows that the sounds changed with age. Adults made a low, loud sound similar to a tuba, while the young ones made higher-pitched squeaks and chirps.

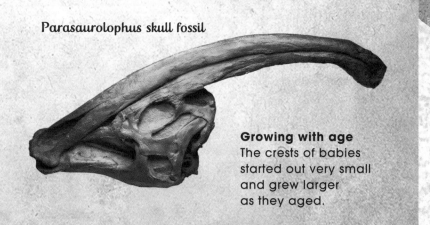

Parasaurolophus skull fossil

Growing with age
The crests of babies started out very small and grew larger as they aged.

Toothless beak
The strong, sharp beak was made of keratin, the same material as bird beaks and turtle shells.

Backwards crest
Hollow tubes leading from each nostril into the skull helped to make sounds, possibly to communicate with others.

Hadrosaurs are called "duck-billed dinosaurs" because their beaks look like the bills of ducks.

Paleobiology of dinosaurs

Fossils aren't just rocks—they are incredible windows into an animal's life history! By looking closely at the inside structure of fossil bone, soft tissues, and coprolites (fossilized poo), we can uncover and understand all sorts of information about extinct animals.

Soft tissue
In 2005, paleontologist Dr. Mary Schweitzer was the first researcher to find real soft tissues from inside the thigh bone of a T. rex nicknamed "B-rex."

Fossil poo
What can we learn from fossil poo? By looking at coprolites, we can learn about an animal's diet, just like we can with animals today. For example, paleontologist and coprolite expert Dr. Karen Chin and colleagues discovered that some herbivorous dinosaurs (possibly duck-billed dinosaurs) ate rotting wood and crustaceans.

Herbivorous dinosaur coprolite

DINOSAUR GROWTH

How did dinosaurs grow up? By studying fossils from dinosaurs of different ages, we can see how they grew and changed over their lifetimes. This is called ontogeny. For example, we know how Triceratops developed because we have lots of their fossils in museums.

Baby
When it is a baby, Triceratops horns are short, pointy, and straight.

Juvenile
As Triceratops grows, its horns grow too, and begin to curve upwards.

Brains

What did dinosaur brains look like? Unfortunately, soft, squishy brains aren't preserved as fossils. Instead, we study endocasts—casts of the spaces where soft body parts used to be. They can be formed from sediments that have naturally filled in the space, cast out of plastic, or created on a computer.

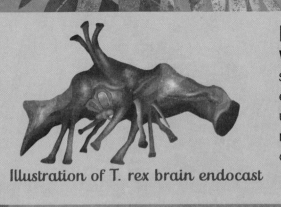

Illustration of T. rex brain endocast

Brain

Thigh bone

Male or female dinosaur?

Female birds and dinosaurs lay eggs made of a mineral called calcium carbonate. They must eat more calcium while they are making eggs so that they don't have to use minerals from their own bones. This extra calcium is stored in special tissue in their thigh bones called medullary tissue. We know that when a fossil contains this tissue it is female. B-rex, the first T. rex to be found with this tissue, was discovered in 2000.

Subadult
As Triceratops nears adult size, its horns get straighter.

Adult
When it is a fully-grown adult, its horns have curved forward and holes have developed in the frill.

53

Hell Creek Formation

This geologic formation is one of the best-preserved ecosystems from the Late Cretaceous in the world. Spreading across northern states of the US, including Montana, the area is rich in dinosaur fossils such as Tyrannosaurus rex and Edmontosaurus.

Pterosaur

CREEK LIFE
A warm sea that ran through North America made this area hot and swampy. Dinosaurs, pterosaurs, crocodiles, and turtles were common.

Redwood forest

Triceratops

Dromaeosaur

Ankylosaurus

Pachycephalosaurus

Fern

Montana badlands
Montana in the US is one of the best places to find Hell Creek Formation fossils. Studying the layers of shale, mudstone, and sandstone that make up the landscape, as well as the fossils locked within them, can help us learn more about this ecosystem 66–68 million years ago.

Cottonwood tree

Purgatorius

Edmontosaurus

Tyrannosaurus rex

Gingko

Tulip tree

55

Cretaceous oceans

With giant fish, plesiosaurs, and mosasaurs, the oceans during the Cretaceous Period were teeming with life. They were full of giant marine reptiles, predatory fish, sharks, diving birds, and car-sized sea turtles.

Elasmosaurus
This plesiosaur lived 80 million years ago and had a neck that was an incredible 23 ft (7 m) long!

Plesiosaurs
Plesiosaurs, such as Elasmosaurus, ruled the Cretaceous oceans. Many of these giant, carnivorous reptiles had long necks, pointed teeth, and large flippers to power themselves through the water.

Elasmosaurus

Fish
Cretaceous fish, such as Xiphactinus, could reach huge sizes. This 16–20 ft (5–6 m)–long fish had a voracious appetite. Several fossils of fish as long as 6.5 ft (2 m) inside the Xiphactinus' stomach have been found in Kansas, US.

Xiphactinus

Tylosaurus
This mosasaur grew to 40 ft (12 m) long. Extra rows of teeth on the roof of its mouth helped it hold slippery prey.

Diving birds

Hesperornis was a bird, but it didn't fly. To catch its dinner, it would dive underwater and grab fish with its razor-sharp teeth.

Hesperornis

Cretoxyrhina

CRETACEOUS SEAWAY

During this period, the continent of North America was split into two by a sea called the Western Interior Seaway. This sea was warm and shallow, making the climate tropical and humid.

Western Interior Seaway

Sharks

Sharks are ancient animals, and date back 440 million years! Cretoxyrhina was a shark as big as a great white shark. It ate anything it could find, including mosasaurs, pterosaurs, dinosaurs, and even diving birds.

Giant turtles

Sea turtles first evolved in the Jurassic Period, 150 million years ago. Archelon, the largest sea turtle, could grow to be 15 ft (4.6 m) long and weigh up to 4.5 tons (4 tonnes).

Archelon

Mosasaurs

Often mistaken for dinosaurs, these giant marine reptiles are more closely related to snakes. Most had sharp teeth for catching prey, while others had round, flat teeth for crushing shells.

Tylosaurus

When the dinosaurs died

66 million years ago, the largest land animals to ever live went extinct. This huge mass extinction wiped out all nonavian (nonflying) dinosaurs, ammonites, flying reptiles, marine reptiles, and many more. It is known as the Cretaceous-Paleogene, or K–Pg, extinction.

Ankylosaurus

Extinction of T. rex
Tyrannosaurus rex was one of the last nonavian dinosaurs on Earth.

Triceratops

Tyrannosaurus rex

75% of life was wiped out in this extinction.

What caused the extinction?

A crater in the Yucatan Peninsula in Mexico is evidence that a massive asteroid hit and wiped out most life on Earth. Scientists also think that volcanoes in the Deccan Traps, an area in India, had been erupting for millions of years before this. Their toxic eruptions were thought to have contributed to climate change across the world, causing wildlife to die out over millions of years.

Pterosaur

Dragonflies

Tardigrade

Scavengers
Birds survived, probably
due to their small size, the
fact they could fly, and
their diet—they ate seeds,
insects, and scavenged.

Birds

GREATEST SURVIVORS
Tardigrades are the only creatures
known to have survived all five
mass extinctions. These microscopic
invertebrates can withstand toxins,
radiation, and dehydration, and
can even survive in outer space.

Lizard

Surviving without food
Crocodilians slowed down
their metabolism so that
they could go for months
without food.

Fungi

The survivors
No land animal more
than 55 lb (25 kg), about the
weight of a bulldog, avoided
extinction. Only the strongest,
most adaptable creatures
survived, including crocodiles,
frogs, and lizards. Birds were
the only dinosaurs to survive.

Frog

Crocodile

59

AFTER THE DINOSAURS

After the Cretaceous-Paleogene extinction, mammals had the opportunity to shine, evolving and adapting to fill the spaces once occupied by dinosaurs.

Mammals are all around us—just take a look in the mirror and you'll see a mammal staring back at you! Humans are part of the group of animals called mammals. From the largest animals on land to ocean-going swimmers and everything in between, mammals have gradually conquered the planet.

Read on to discover more about the group of animals you belong to.

Ashfall Fossil Beds State Historical Park in Antelope County, Nebraska, US
This fossil site is famous for the hundreds of rhinoceros fossils preserved by volcanic ash following a volcanic eruption 13–11 million years ago.

The age of mammals

After the asteroid impact that killed off the dinosaurs, animals and plants slowly began to recover in a new age: the Cenozoic Era. Mammals that had lived in the Mesozoic Era were never larger than a raccoon. But without dinosaurs around, mammals could come out from the shadows and thrive in new habitats during the Cenozoic Era.

Plesiadapis

Taeniolabis

Gastornis

Ceratodus

Inkayacu

Knightia

Eohippus

Basilosaurus

Ulintatherium

Paleoparadoxia

Dromornis

Hoplophoneus

Daeodon

Baleen whale

PALEOCENE PERIOD (66–56 MYA)

The climate was hot and tropical with no ice sheets at the poles. Without large herbivores, forests flourished. Small multituberculates (rodentlike mammals) such as Taeniolabis were the most successful group of mammals during this period. Many modern birds can be traced back to this time.

EOCENE PERIOD (56–33 MYA)

Due to volcanoes erupting, the climate was the warmest it had been since the Permian-Triassic extinction. The average temperature was 72–82°F (22–28°C). Palm trees grew in tropical polar regions. Ancestors of hoofed animals, such as the ancient horse Eohippus, were small. Pythons, crocodilians, and turtles were plentiful.

OLIGOCENE PERIOD (33–23 MYA)

As the climate began to cool, ice sheets formed at the poles and sea levels dropped. Climate change caused tropical forests to get smaller, while grasslands expanded, giving early horses, rhinos, and camels space to run. Predators had to learn and adapt new ways to keep up.

Humans evolved in the Pleistocene. They began as apes and slowly developed the ability to stand upright, make tools, and use language.

HOLOCENE PERIOD (11,700 YA–PRESENT)

The Holocene, or Anthropocene, is the age we are currently in. While most of the huge animals of the Ice Age have died out, there are still some incredible animals whose beginnings date back to after the extinction of the dinosaurs. As humans, we can use what we learn about all of the time periods before us to take care of the world in the future.

Pelagornis

Gomphotherium

Purussaurus

Amphicyon

Glyptodont

Australopithecus afarensis

Megatherium

Otodus megalodon

Woolly mammoth

Gigantopithecus

Homo sapiens

Megalania

MIOCENE PERIOD (23–5 MYA)

This period was warm, but the climate was still cooling down. Grasslands spread and big herds of grass-grazers, such as piglike oreodonts, grew with them. Bone-crushing bear dogs, such as Amphicyon, and proboscideans (elephant relatives), such as Gomphotherium, evolved.

PLIOCENE PERIOD (5–2 MYA)

The climate of the Pliocene Period was a little warmer than our climate today. South America and North America became connected by a narrow strip of land, called the Isthmus of Panama. This new land bridge between the continents allowed animals, including the giant ground sloth Megatherium and armadillo Glyptodont, to migrate.

PLEISTOCENE PERIOD (2 MILLION–11,000 YA)

This period is also known as the Ice Age. Many northern parts of the world were covered in massive ice sheets. There were many ice ages throughout the Pleistocene. In this period, humans (Homo sapiens) and huge mammals such as the woolly mammoth and Gigantopithecus, a giant ape, evolved.

Woolly mammoth

While humans did not live at the same time as dinosaurs, they lived with and hunted mammoths for survival. These hairy beasts roamed the snowy northern tundra in herds during the Ice Age.

Toothy tusks
Baby mammoths were born with tusks that kept growing throughout their lives. Tusks look like horns, but they are actually two giant teeth called incisors, like your front teeth.

Woolly mammoth

CAVE ART

Early humans would draw animals on rock or cave walls. These drawings help us understand what animals looked like at the time. For example, we know that woolly mammoths had fatty humps on the tops of their heads and on their shoulders.

Sensitive trunk
The trunk is a mammoth's nose and upper lip. It is used for smelling, breathing, feeling, and grasping.

Surviving the cold

Woolly mammoths were covered in two layers of thick, brown fur. This helped them stay warm in the freezing Ice Age climate.

Woolly coat
Paleontologists have found mammoth hair still frozen in ice!

BACK FROM THE DEAD

By studying mammoths preserved in ice, scientists have been able to extract their DNA—the genetic information that makes them what they are. Scientists are using the DNA to understand them, and maybe even bring them back from extinction. The question is: should scientists bring back woolly mammoths from extinction or focus on protecting endangered animals, such as their cousins, Asian elephants?

Why did they go extinct?

Mammoths went extinct along with other huge Ice Age mammals at the end of the Pleistocene Period. We are still trying to understand the causes, but climate change and hunting by humans both played a role.

Cenozoic giants

Following the Cretaceous-Paleogene extinction, many animals gradually grew to gargantuan sizes once more. From the largest shark that ever lived to the enormous whale that still exists today, the Cenozoic Era boasted some of the largest animals of all time.

Size
Max weight: 1,610 lb (730 kg)
Max length: 42 ft (13 m)

THE BIG AND BIZARRE

Dinosaurs weren't the only huge animals to walk the Earth. In fact, many of the animals in the Cenozoic Era were even larger and even weirder! The ones on this page lived at different times throughout the era.

Titanoboa

The Cenozoic Era may have been the age of mammals, but this massive reptile ruled. This supersized boa constrictor was large enough to eat giant fish, turtles, and even whole crocodiles. It lived 60–58 million years ago.

Blue whale

The largest animal to have ever existed is still alive today. The blue whale is a filter-feeding baleen whale. It takes in large amounts of seawater and filters it for krill (shrimplike sea creatures).

Size
Max weight: 110 tons (100 tonnes)
Max length: 100 ft (30 m)

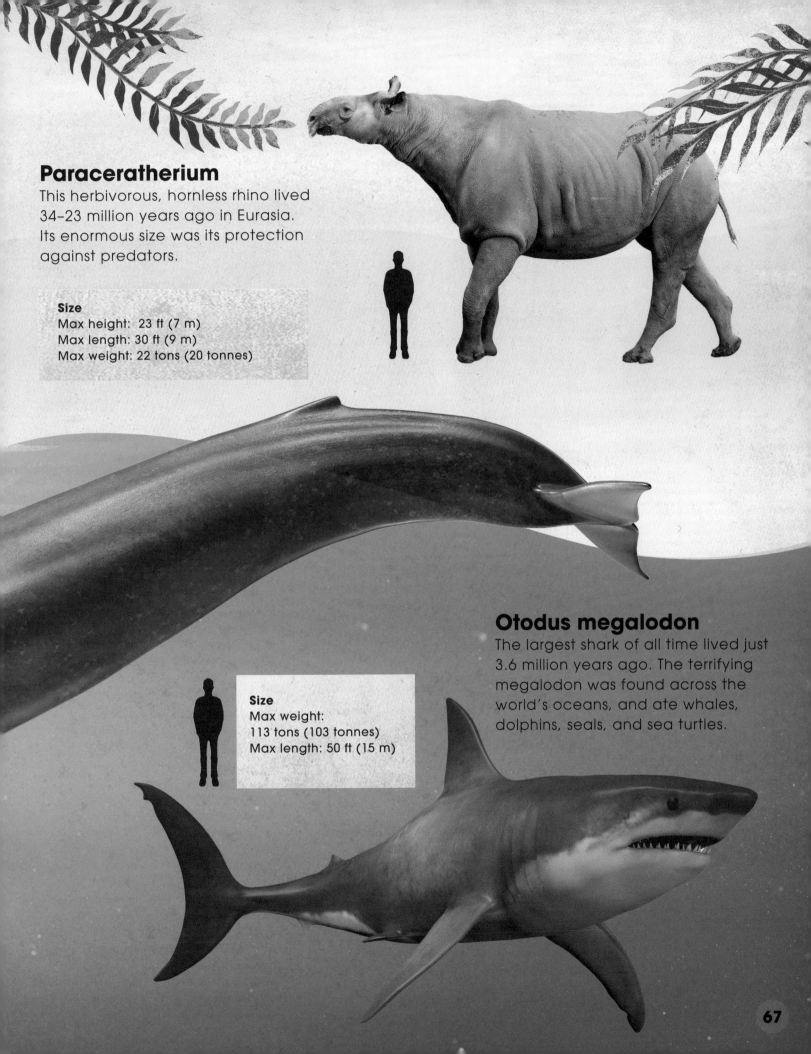

Paraceratherium

This herbivorous, hornless rhino lived 34–23 million years ago in Eurasia. Its enormous size was its protection against predators.

Size
Max height: 23 ft (7 m)
Max length: 30 ft (9 m)
Max weight: 22 tons (20 tonnes)

Otodus megalodon

The largest shark of all time lived just 3.6 million years ago. The terrifying megalodon was found across the world's oceans, and ate whales, dolphins, seals, and sea turtles.

Size
Max weight:
113 tons (103 tonnes)
Max length: 50 ft (15 m)

PREHISTORIC WORLDS AND ME

Who can be a paleontologist? You can! Studying fossils is not only fun, but it's possible to do in so many different ways—there is not just one path to becoming a paleontologist.

Paleontology has only been around as a science for about 200 years. As you already know by reading this book, organisms have been evolving on Earth for **3.5 billion years**, so we have only just begun to discover them.

So, by the time you become a paleontologist, there will be many **amazing fossil discoveries** still to be made—and some of them could be made by you!

Read on to learn how you can become a paleontologist and study prehistoric worlds.

From the field to the lab

Fossils are thousands to millions of years old, so they can be very fragile. Paleontologists spend a few months of every year digging up fossils. This is called fieldwork. Fieldwork involves a variety of things, from understanding where to look for fossils, to transporting them, to cleaning them, to finally storing them safely.

Looking for fossils is called prospecting.

Fieldwork: finding fossils

Paleontogists can't just start digging—they have to know where to go! For example, Spinosaurus and T. rex aren't found in the same place or time. T. rex lived 66–68 million years ago in North America, while Spinosaurus lived 99–93 million years ago in Egypt. Geologic maps show layers of the Earth's surface and their ages. Mapping can help paleontologists work out where a particular fossil might be, while fossils on the surface of the ground are a sign that more might be found underground.

Fossil preparation: cleaning fossils

Fossils have to be treated with great care. Once they are brought back to the museum, paleontologists called fossil preparators open each fossil's wrapping carefully. Using small hand tools, such as picks, and larger electric hand tools, they gently pick away at the dirt and rock surrounding the fossil. Once the fossil is exposed, they use special glues to repair cracks and breaks.

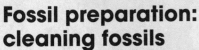

Collections management: storing fossils

After a fossil has been cleaned, it is given a number and stored in metal drawers in special cabinets. There, they are kept safely by the paleontology collections manager.

Fossils stored in drawers

Research: studying fossils

Every fossil found adds to a collection that helps researchers answer questions. More fossils, more answers! For example, the more of one species researchers have, the more information there is about how it grew up, changed throughout its life, and the diseases it may have had.

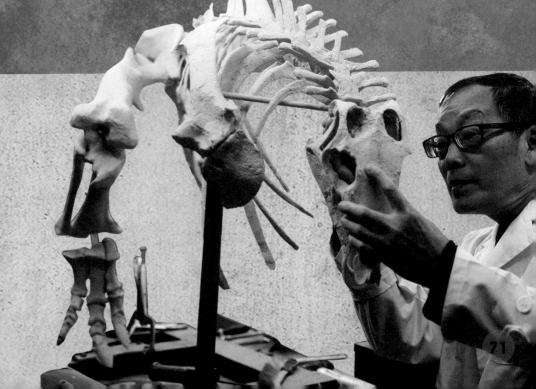

21

What's left to learn?

Since paleontology has only been a science for 200 years, we have so much still to learn! As new technology evolves, we find new ways to study fossils, and we've only scratched the surface of what there is to know about prehistoric worlds.

What did dinosaurs sound like?

Birds and crocodiles are the closest living relatives to dinosaurs. We can look at the way they communicate to help us imagine the sounds that dinosaurs made. For example, dinosaurs probably didn't roar like mammals, because mammals have very different vocal cords from birds and crocodiles.

Giving birth
Being able to give birth to live young meant plesiosaurs did not need to crawl onto land to lay eggs.

Did any dinosaurs give birth to live young?

Fossils of plesiosaurs and ichthyosaurs, marine reptiles, have been found with developing babies still inside the females, showing us they gave birth to their babies instead of laying eggs. Although we know that most dinosaurs laid eggs, we are still trying to find out if any had live young like these other prehistoric creatures.

What did T. rex and Triceratops eggs look like?

While eggs have been found from some theropods and ceratopsians, we have not yet found eggs from two of the most famous dinosaurs in the world: T. rex and Triceratops.

Why didn't any nonavian dinosaurs survive the extinction?

We still don't know! Birds are the only dinosaurs that survived the extinction, but we're not sure why no other small nonavian dinosaurs survived.

HOW FAR WE'VE COME

We are constantly making discoveries about life on Earth millions of years ago. A new species of dinosaur (Vectipelta barretti) was discovered as recently as 2023. However, there are still many questions that paleontologists have yet to answer...

What did dinosaur guts look like?

Bones and skin fossilize, but not internal organs. What did a dinosaur's heart look like? Did dinosaurs have a crop (pouch in the throat for food) like birds or just a stomach?

What color were dinosaurs?

We know how to analyze color in feathered dinosaurs, but not in nonavian dinosaurs. So when you're doing your coloring-in, you can still use your imagination!

Careers in paleontology

So you want to be a paleontologist? Great! There are plenty of paths you can take to get into paleontology—you are already on your way just by reading this book. Here are just a few of the jobs that will allow you to work with fossils.

Handle with care
Collections managers clean and preserve fragile fossils for the future.

Know your stuff
Educators read lots of books and journals to learn about exciting new fossil discoveries.

An eye for detail
Magnifying glasses help curators see tiny details when examining fossils.

CURATOR

The people who are in charge of the paleontology departments in museums are curators. Their varied roles range from organizing summer field expeditions to unearth new specimens to researching and publishing studies about their discoveries.

COLLECTIONS MANAGER

These managers are like librarians, but instead of looking after books, they keep fossils safe in special drawers and cabinets for study. Fossil collections are stored in places such as museums and national parks.

EDUCATOR

The main purpose of this role is to teach people about prehistory and fossils. From working in a museum to being a university professor, being an educator allows you to tell others about what you love. You may even inspire someone to seek a career in paleontology!

PALEOARTIST

These special artists reconstruct what fossils and extinct life would have looked like. They use many different forms of art, from drawing and painting to sculpting and digital animation.

PARK RANGER

Park rangers and government paleontologists work to protect and preserve fossils that are on public land such as badlands and deserts.

MITIGATOR

Paleontology mitigators work at building sites to recover and save fossils when construction workers are digging.

Tools of the trade
Field bags are packed with tools.

PREPARATOR

This role involves caring for fossils using special tools. Picks, brushes, air pens, and more are used to carefully separate fossils from rocks. Preparators are experts in fossil preservation, even making special glues to repair fragile fossils.

HOW TO BECOME A PALEONTOLOGIST

There is not just one route you can take into paleontology, but following these simple steps is a good place to start on your paleontology journey:

1. Stay curious—keep learning, reading, and asking questions.
2. Visit museums—take trips to museums and try to see fossils wherever you go.
3. Study hard—pay attention in your science classes at school!
4. Reach out—get in touch with paleontologists you admire or those at your local museums or universities. They like talking to fossil fans like you!

Glossary

ADAPT
How a living thing changes over time to help it survive better in its environment.

AIR PEN
Fossil preparation tool which cleans fossils with a jet of air.

ANCESTOR
Animal or plant to which a more recent one is related.

ARTHROPOD
Group of invertebrates with tough outer skeletons and bodies divided into segments.

AVIAN
Relating to birds.

BYA
Stands for "billion years ago."

CATALOG
Make a list of items.

CLIMATE CHANGE
Change in temperature and weather across the Earth that can have a variety of causes, from natural ones to the effects of human activity.

CROP
Part of the digestive system in birds, which stores food after it has been swallowed.

DIVERSIFY
Become more varied.

ECOSYSTEM
Community of living things and their nonliving environment, including the soil, water, and air around them.

ENDANGERED
At risk of becoming extinct.

EROSION
Changes in the surface of the Earth as features get worn away by the weather.

EVOLVE
The way living things change and adapt over time to help them survive.

EXTINCT
When a plant or animal species has disappeared forever

EXTINCTION EVENT
When a large amount of Earth's living things die in a short period of time.

GENETIC
Relating to the origins of a living thing.

GREENHOUSE GAS
Gas in Earth's atmosphere that traps heat, like a greenhouse.

HERBIVORE
Animal that eats only plants.

INVERTEBRATE
Animal that does not have a backbone.

MARINE
Found in the sea.

MOLLUSK
Animal with a soft body, and often a hard shell, such as a clam.

MYA
Stands for "million years ago."

NOCTURNAL
Active at night.

ORGANISM
Living thing.

PERMAFROST
Layer of permanently frozen soil underground.

SCAVENGE
Gather or search an area for food.

SEDIMENT
Material, such as mud and sand, made from ground down natural materials.

SIBERIAN TRAPS
Region of volcanic rock in what is now Siberia, Russia, that was formed from many massive volcanic eruptions.

SOFT TISSUE
Soft materials in the body such as muscles, fat, and blood vessels

TUNDRA
Cold, treeless area where soil remains frozen.

UK GEOLOGICAL SOCIETY
Based in London in the UK and founded in 1807.

GEOLOGICAL SOCIETY OF AMERICA
Based in Boulder, Colorado, and founded in 1888.

Geologists join geological societies to learn about geology and share their findings.

VERTEBRATE
Animal that has a backbone.

Index

Pronunciation guide

Aetosaur
Ay-toe-sor

Allosaurus
Al-oh-sor-us

Amphicyon
Am-fee-si-on

Ankylosaurus
Ank-ill-oh-sor-us

Apatosaurus
A-pat-oh-sor-us

Araeoscelis
A-ray-oh-skel-is

Archaeopteryx
Ar-key-op-ter-ix

Archean
Ar-key-uhn

Archelon
Ar-kell-on

Archosaur
Ar-koh-sor

Atopodentatus
A-top-oh-den-tah-tus

Australopithecus afarensis
Os-tra-low-pith-ee-cuss
a-far-en-sis

Basilosaurus
Bah-sil-oh-sor-us

Brachiopod
Bra-key-oh-pod

Brachiosaurus
Bra-key-oh-sor-us

Cambrian
Kam-bree-uhn

Cenozoic
See-no-zo-ik

Ceratodus
Seh-ra-to-dus

Ceratopsian
Seh-ra-tops-ee-uhn

Coelophysis
See-low-fye-sis

Coronodon
Cor-on-oh-don

Cotylorhynchus
Co-tye-low-rin-kus

Cretaceous
Creh-tay-shuss

Cretoxyrhina
Creh-tox-ee-rye-nah

Cymbospondylus youngorum
Sim-bo-spon-dil-lus
yung-or-um

Cynodont
Si-no-dont

Daeodon
Day-oh-don

Dapedium politum
Da-pee-de-um pol-it-um

Devonian
De-vo-nee-uhn

Dicynodont
Die-sy-no-dont

Dimetrodon
Die-met-roe-don

Dimorphodon macronyx
Die-mor-foe-don mak-ron-ix

Dinocephalian
Die-no-seh-fay-lee-uhn

Diplocaulus
Dip-low-call-us

Diplodocus
Dip-lod-oh-kuss

Drepanosaurus
Dre-pan-oh-sor-us

Dromornis
Druh-mor-nis

Echinoderm
Ee-kye-no-derm

Edaphosaurus
Ee-daf-oh-sor-us

Edmontosaurus
Ed-mont-oh-sor-us

Elasmosaurus
E-laz-moe-sor-us

Elephantosaurus
E-le-fan-toe-sor-us

Eocene
Ee-oh-seen

Eohippus
Ee-oh-hip-uhs

Eoraptor
Ee-oh-rap-tor

Ericiolacerta
E-re-cee-o-lah-ser-tah

Eryops
E-ree-ops

Estemmenosuchus
Es-teh-men-oh-soo-kus

Eudimorphodon
Yoo-die-mor-foe-don

Falcatus
Fal-kat-us

Gastornis
Gas-tor-nis

Gerrothorax
Ge-ro-thor-ax

Gigantopithecus
Ji-gan-toe-pith-eck-us

Gigantspinosaurus
Ji-gant-spy-noe-sor-us

Glyptodont
Glip-toe-dont

Gomphotherium
Gom-foe-thee-ree-um

Goniatite
Go-nee-at-ite

Hadrocodium
Had-row-co-dee-um

Hadrosaur
Had-row-sor

Helicoprion
Hel-ee-co-pree-on

Herrerasaurus
Heh-rare-ra-sor-us

Hesperornis
Hes-per-or-nis

Holocene
Ho-luh-seen

Hoplophoneus
Hop-low-foe-nee-us

Hypsilophodon
Hip-sih-loaf-oh-don

Ichthyosaur
Ik-thee-oh-sor

Iguanodon
Ig-wah-no don

Inkayacu
In-kye-ah-koo

Inostrancevia
In-oh-stran-see-vee-ah

Knightia
Nite-ee-ah

Leedsichthys
Leeds-ik this

Lepidodendron
Lep-i-do-den-dron

Liopleurodon
Lie-oh-ploor-oh-don

Lystrosaurus
Lis-trow-sor-us

Marella splendens
Ma-rel-ah splen-dens

Marginocephalian
Mar-ji-no-sa-fay-lee-an

Megalancosaurus
Me-ga-lan-co-sor-us

Megalania
Me-ga-la-nee-ya

Megalodon
Me-ga-low-don

Meganeura
Me-ga-new-ra

Megatherium
Me-ga-theer-ee-um

Megazostrodon
Me-ga-zo-stroh-don

Mesozoic
Mes-oh-zo-ik

Microraptor
My-crow-rap-tor

Miocene
My-oh-seen

Mississippian
Mis-is-ip-ee-un

Morganucodon
Mor-gan-oo-code-on

Mosasaurus
Mose-ah-sor-us

Moschops
Moe-shops

Nothosaurus
No-tho-sor-us

Nyasasaurus
Nye-as-uh-sor-us

Oligocene
Oh-li-go-seen

Ophthalmosaurus
Off-thal-mo-sor-us

Ordovician
Or-doh-vish-ee-uhn

Ornithischian
Or-nith-isk-ee-uhn

Ornithopod
Or-nith-oh-pod

Osteoderm
Os-tee-oh-derm

Otodus megalodon
Oh-toe-dus me-ga-low-don

Pachycephalosaur
Pak-ee-sef-ah-low-sor

Pakicetus
Pak-ee-seh-tus

Paleocene
Pay-lee-oh-seen

Paleoparadoxia
Pay-lee-oh-pah-ra-dox-ee-a

Paleozoic
Pay-lee-oh-zo-ik

Panthalassa
Pan-tha-la-sa

Paraceratherium
Pa-ra-seh-ra-theer-ee-um

Parasaurolophus
Pa-ra-sor-oh-loaf-us

Patagotitan
Pat-ah-go-tie-tan

Pelagornis
Pe-la-gore-niss

Peltobatrachus
Pel-toe-ba-trak-us

Pennsylvanian
Pen-suhl-vay-nee-uhn

Permian
Per-mee-uhn

Phytosaur
Fye-toe-sor

Pisanosaurus
Pis-ah-no-sor-us

Plateosaurus
Plate-ee-oh-sor-us

Pleistocene
Plye-stuh-seen

Plesiadapis
Plee-zee-ah-dap-is

Plesiosaur
Plee-zee-oh-sor

Pleuromeia
Ploo-roh-me-ah

Pliocene
Plye-oh-seen

Pliosaur
Plee-oh-sor

Poposaurs
Pop-oh-sor-us

Precambrian
Pree-cam-bree-an

Prionosuchus
Pree-on-oh-soo-kus

Procoptodon
Pro-cop-toe-don

Proterozoic
Pro-ter-oh-zo-ik

**Protojuniperoxylon
ischigualastianus**
Pro-toe-joo-ni-per-ox-i-lon
ish-ee-gwa-las-tee-an-us

Pseudosuchians
Soo-doe-soo-kee-uns

Pteranodon
Teh-ran-oh-don

Pterodactylus
Teh-roe-dak-til-us

Pterosaur
Teh-roe-sor

Purgatorius
Per-gah-tor-ee-us

Purussaurus
Puh-roo-sor-us

**Rhomaleosaurus
cramptoni**
Ro-mal-ee-oh-sor-us
cramp-toe-nee

Rhynchosaurus
Rin-ko-sor-us

Saurischia
Sor-ris-kee-uhn

Sauropodomorph
Sor-oh-pod-oh-morf

Sauropod
Sor-oh-pod

Saurornitholestes
Sor-oh-nith-oh-les-teez

Scansoriopterygid
Scan-sor-ee-op-ter-i-jid

Silene stenophylla
Si-leen sten-oh-fil-ah

Silesaurus
Si-luh-sor-us

Silurian
Si-loor-ee-an

Sinosauropteryx
Si-no-sor-op-ter-ix

Siriusgnathus
Si-re-us-nay-thus

Smilodon
Smye-lo-don

Soliclymenia
Sol-ee-clye-meen-ee-ah

Spinosaurus
Spine-oh-sor-us

Stegosaurus
Steg-oh-sor-us

Stethacanthus
Steth-a-can-thus

Styracosaurus
Sty-rack-oh-sor-us

Taeniolabis
Tay-nee-oh-lay-bis

Temnospondyls
Tem-no-spon-dils

Therapsids
Thuh-rap-sids

Thyreophoran
Thy-ree-oh-for-an

Tiktaalik roseae
Tik-ta-lik rose-ay

Titanoboa
Tie-tan-oh-bo-a

Triassic
Try-as-ik

Triceratops
Try-seh-ra-tops

Tylosaurus
Tie-low-sor-us

Tyrannosaurus rex
Tie-ran-oh-sor-us rex

Uintatherium
Win-tah-thee-ree-um

Vectipelta barretti
Vec-tee-pel-tah bar-et-ee

Velociraptor
Vel-os-i-rap-tor

Volaticotherium
Vole-at-ee-ko-thee-ree-um

Xiphactinus
Zye-fac-tee-nus

Yi qi
Yee chee

Acknowledgments

The publisher would like to thank the following people for their assistance: Francesca Harper for the pronunciation guide, Karen Chin for use of her images, Helen Peters for the index, and Caroline Hunt for proofreading.

Ashley would like to thank her husband, Lee, and her two cats for their endless love and support.

PICTURE CREDITS

The publisher would like to thank the following for their kind permission to reproduce their photographs: (Key: a-above; b-below/bottom; c-center; f-far; l-left; r-right; t-top)

2 Dorling Kindersley: Colin Keates / Natural History Museum, London (cla). **2-80 Dreamstime.com:** Designprintck (Texture). **3 Dorling Kindersley:** Jon Hughes (tc). **4-5 Alamy Stock Photo:** Lee Rentz. **6 Alamy Stock Photo:** PhotoAlto sas / Jerome Gorin (cb). **Dreamstime.com:** Marcos Souza (clb). **Science Photo Library:** Dirk Wiersma (tr). **7 Alamy Stock Photo:** PRAWNS (tl); Stefan Sollfors (cb). **Getty Images:** Feature China / Future Publishing (clb). **8 Dorling Kindersley:** Colin Keates / Natural History Museum, London (cb, tr). **9 Science Photo Library:** Millard H. Sharp (tc). **11 Dreamstime.com:** Onestar (tl). **12 123RF.com:** Mark Turner (tr). **13 Dreamstime.com:** Isselee (tr). **14-15 Alamy Stock Photo:** Roland Bouvier. **16 Shutterstock.com:** Dotted Yeti (clb, cb). **16-17 Dreamstime.com:** Mark Turner (t). **17 Dreamstime.com:** Elena Duvernay (cr); Corey A Ford (tr); Mark Turner (clb). **18 Science Photo Library:** Millard H. Sharp (clb). **20-21 Dreamstime.com:** Alexander Ogurtsov (cb). **20 Alamy Stock Photo:** Hypersphere / Science Photo Library (clb). **Dorling Kindersley:** Colin Keates / Natural History Museum, London (br). **21 naturepl.com:** Alex Mustard (crb). **22-23 Dreamstime.com:** Linda Bucklin (c). **23 Dreamstime.com:** Victor Zherebtsov (tr). **25 Alamy Stock Photo:** Corbin17 (bc); Natural History Museum, London (tl, tr, br); Custom Life Science Images (bl). **Science Photo Library:** Kjell B. Sandved (tc). **26 123RF.com:** Corey A Ford (tr). **28-29 Alamy Stock Photo:** Jamie Pham. **30 123RF.com:** Corey A Ford (cra). **Dorling Kindersley:** Jon Hughes (br). **31 Alamy Stock Photo:** Mohamad Haghani (cr). **Dorling Kindersley:** James Kuether (crb). **Getty Images:** Moment / John Finney

Photography (br). **32 Dorling Kindersley:** Jon Hughes (clb). **37 Dorling Kindersley:** Jon Hughes (tl). **38 Dreamstime.com:** Mark Turner (cl). **42-43 Dreamstime.com:** Cornelius20. **Shutterstock.com:** SciePro (c). **44 Dorling Kindersley:** Colin Keates / Natural History Museum, London (t). **44-45 Dreamstime.com:** Elena Duvernay (c). **45 123RF.com:** Michael Rosskothen (cra). **Science Photo Library:** Julius T Csotonyi (cr). **46 Alamy Stock Photo:** IanDagnall Computing (bl). **Shutterstock.com:** Simon J Beer. **47 Alamy Stock Photo:** David Buzzard (bl). **Science Photo Library:** Natural History Museum, London (tc). **48 123RF.com:** Corey A Ford (c). **Alamy Stock Photo:** Mark Garlick / Science Photo Library (cla). **Dorling Kindersley:** Jon Hughes (tc). **49 123RF.com:** Leonello Calvetti (cr); Corey A Ford (clb). **Dorling Kindersley:** Jon Hughes (tl); James Kuether (bc). **50 123RF.com:** Mark Turner (ca). **Getty Images / iStock:** DmitriyKazitsyn (cl). **51 123RF.com:** Mark Turner (br). **Dorling Kindersley:** Colin Keates / Natural History Museum, London (tr). **52 Photo by Karen Chin;** specimen from the collections of the Denver Museum of Nature and Science: (cl). **54 123RF.com:** Leonello Calvetti (cr). **Alamy Stock Photo:** Tim Fitzharris / Minden Pictures (bl). **57 Alamy Stock Photo:** Sebastian Kaulitzki / Science Photo Library (crb). **Shutterstock.com:** SciePro (cb). **58 123RF.com:** Leonello Calvetti (cl). **59 Dreamstime.com:** Alslutsky (cr). **Shutterstock.com:** Dotted Yeti (tr). **60-61 Alamy Stock Photo:** Jim West. **62 123RF.com:** Ralf KRaft (cr). **Alamy Stock Photo:** Universal Images Group North America LLC / DeAgostini (cla). **Dreamstime.com:** William Roberts (clb). **Science Photo Library:** Roman Uchytel (cra). **Shutterstock.com:** SciePro (c). **63 Dorling Kindersley:** Dynamo (cla). **Dreamstime.com:** Corey A Ford (ca). **Getty Images / iStock:** CoreyFord (cb). **Science Photo Library:** John Bavaro Fine Art (cra). **64 Alamy Stock Photo:** GRANGER - Historical Picture Archive (clb). **65 Alamy Stock Photo:** Science Picture Co (tr). **66-67 Getty Images / iStock:** DigitalVision Vectors / aelitta (Silhouettes). **66 Alamy Stock Photo:** Friedrich Saurer (ca). **67 Getty Images / iStock:** CoreyFord (b). **Science Photo Library:** Roman Uchytel (tr). **68-69 Alamy Stock Photo:** Brusini Aurlien / Hemis.fr. **71 Alamy Stock Photo:** Qin Tingfu / Xinhua (br); Bodo Schackow / dpa-Zentralbild / ZB (cla). **Getty Images:** Moment / Jordi Salas (tr). **74 Shutterstock.com:** PolinaPersikova (cl). **75 Getty Images / iStock:** fares139 (cla). **Science Photo Library:** Pascal Goetgheluck (crb)

Cover images: *Front:* **123RF.com:** Leonello Calvetti cr, Corey A Ford ca, Mark Turner tl; **Dorling Kindersley:** Andy Crawford / Roby Braun clb, Jon Hughes cl; **Dreamstime.com:** Designprintck (Texture), Mark Turner crb; **Getty Images / iStock:** CoreyFord cla; *Back:* **123RF.com:** Leonello Calvetti cl, Corey A Ford ca, Mark Turner tr; **Dorling Kindersley:** Andy Crawford / Roby Braun crb, Jon Hughes cr; **Dreamstime.com:** Designprintck (Texture), Mark Turner clb; **Getty Images / iStock:** CoreyFord cra

All other images © Dorling Kindersley

ABOUT THE ILLUSTRATOR

Claire McElfatrick is a freelance artist. Her beautiful hand-drawn and collaged illustrations are inspired by her home in rural England. Claire has illustrated all the other books in this series: *The Magic and Mystery of Trees, The Book of Brilliant Bugs, Earth's Incredible Oceans, The Extraordinary World of Birds* and *The Frozen Worlds.*